Timed Reading for Fluency

Timed Reading for Fluency 1

Paul Nation / Casey Malarcher

© 2017 Seed Learning, Inc.
7212 Canary Lane,
Sachse, TX, USA

Acquisitions Editor: Kelly Daniels
Content Editor: David Charlton
Copy Editor: Andrea Janzen
Design: Highline Studio

The authors would like to acknowledge Kelly Lee, Randy Lewis, and Joy Yongo for contributing material to this book.

http://www.seed-learning.com

ISBN: 978-1-9464-5267-2

10 9 8 7 6 5 4 3 2
21 20 19 18 17

Photo Credits

Timed Reading for Fluency

Paul Nation / Casey Malarcher

Seed
Learning

Contents

Introduction

A well-organized language course provides opportunities for learning through communicative activities involving listening, speaking, reading and writing, deliberate study, and fluency development. The fluency development part of a course should take about one-quarter of the course time, and there should be fluency development activities for each of the four skills of listening, speaking, reading, and writing.

This series of books focuses on fluency in reading. Fluency involves making the best use of what you already know. That comes from working with familiar vocabulary and grammar, and from practicing using them in a comfortable way without having to struggle.

Four Requirements of Fluency Development:

1. Familiar Material

Material for fluency development must be known and familiar. It should not involve unfamiliar language items or content too far removed from what learners already know. This is because to become fluent, learners need to focus on using material they already know well, not on learning new vocabulary or grammar. This is why the texts in these books are grouped into topic areas so that learners can read several texts about very similar information. Their familiarity with the topic will help them increase their reading speed.

Learners do not get fluent in reading by struggling through difficult texts with lots of unknown words. The books in this series are carefully written within a controlled vocabulary so that there is a minimum of unknown words. Words that might be unfamiliar to some learners are dealt with before the reading texts.

2. Quantity of Practice

Another key requirement of a fluency development course is quantity of practice. Fluency develops by doing plenty of practice with easy material. That is why each book in this series contains a lot of reading texts. When learners have finished working through one book in the series, it is a good idea if they go back over the texts they have already read, trying to read them faster than they did the first time.

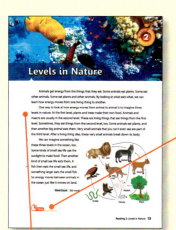

3. Pressure to Go Faster

A fluency development course will work well if there is some pressure to go faster when using the language. This series of books uses timed readings. When the learners read, they measure how long it takes them to do the reading, and they keep a record of their reading speed. Their aim is to increase their speed until it gets close to 250 words per minute. The upper limit of reading speed is 300 words per minute. Reading faster than that requires skipping words on the page and relying on background knowledge to fill the gaps. While this is a useful reading skill, it does not help develop reading fluency in a second language.

Book 1 is written within a vocabulary of 800 words, Book 2 within 1,100 words, Book 3 within 1,500 words, and Book 4 within 2,000 words.

4. A Focus on Comprehension

Fluency in reading not only involves speed of word recognition, but also involves comprehension. This is why the texts in these books are followed by questions. There is no value in reading faster if there is a big drop in comprehension.

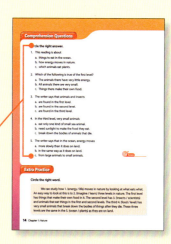

At the back of each book there is a graph where learners should enter their reading speed for each text and their comprehension score. The learners' goal should be to make their reading speed graph keep going up.

Chapter 1

Nature

A **Look at the pictures. Write the right words.**

Aloe vera	careful	Dolphins	health
scientist	smart	suddenly	Tornadoes

1. _____ are very _____ animals.

2. _____ can _____ hit trees and houses.

3. Some people use _____ plants for their _____.

4. The _____ writes _____ notes about an animal he sees.

B Match the meaning with the right word.

1. _____ very quickly; without warning   a. cloud

2. _____ knowing a lot; intelligent   b. breathe

3. _____ a big white thing in the sky   c. health

4. _____ how good or bad your body is   d. suddenly

5. _____ to make air go into and out of the body e. smart

C Work with a classmate. Think about things in nature. Write two ideas for plants or animals that . . .

1. . . . can be used for one's health.

   _____

2. . . . are able to breathe in water.

   _____

3. . . . are dangerous, so you must be careful near them.

   _____

4. . . . won't be hurt when a tornado hits.

   _____

D Read about different plants and animals. Write the right word in each blank.

Raintrees	Aloe Vera	Bluebirds	River Dolphins

1. _____ 2. _____ 3. _____ 4. _____

• are green • can be eaten • have a chemical that is good for our skin	• are not common around the world • breathe air • swim in lakes and rivers	• look for food during the day • can sing • lay blue eggs	• grow in South America • close their leaves at night • have nice wood for furniture

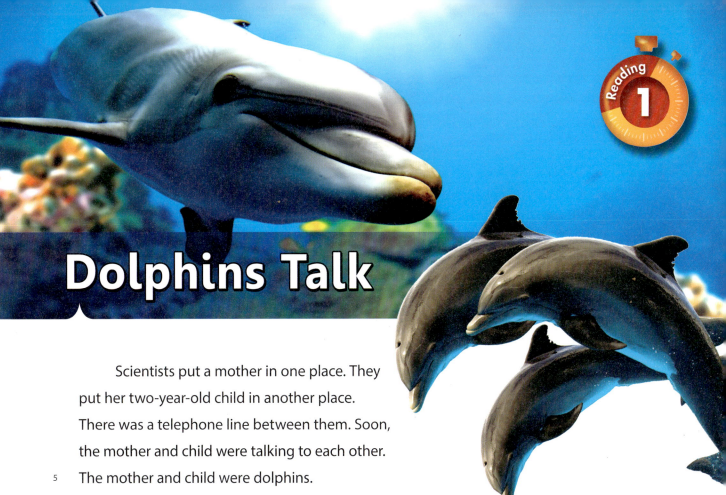

Dolphins Talk

Scientists put a mother in one place. They
put her two-year-old child in another place.
There was a telephone line between them. Soon,
the mother and child were talking to each other.
5 The mother and child were dolphins.

In this test, one of the two dolphins would make
a sound. Then the other dolphin would make the same sound.
Also, the scientists believed that the two animals knew who they were talking to.

Scientists have known for a long time that animals can "talk" with each other. But
10 dolphins have a special way of talking. And they are very smart. When they are in a group,
they "talk" to each other. They do this using different sounds. Scientists have listened to
the dolphins' sounds, and they have watched the dolphins. They now believe that the
dolphins really are talking. They just don't know what the dolphins are saying.

Dolphins not only use sounds. They use body language, too. They "tell" something
15 to another dolphin by moving their body in a special way. They also do it by opening and
closing their mouths quickly.

Scientists hope to understand dolphin language. They want to learn more about
these very interesting animals.

Word Count   200 words

 Time _____

Comprehension Questions

Circle the right answer.

1. This reading is about
   a. dolphins that talk to people.
   b. dolphins that talk to each other.
   c. dolphins that talk to fish.

2. Scientists believe that the mother dolphin and her baby
   a. were just making noise.
   b. were talking about other dolphins.
   c. knew who they were talking to.

3. Which of these is NOT a way dolphins talk?
   a. By using their bodies
   b. By using other fish
   c. By using sounds

4. Dolphins are special animals because
   a. they can "talk" to other animals.
   b. they have a special language.
   c. they understand human speech.

5. Besides using sounds to "talk," dolphins tell things to each other by
   a. pushing water quickly or slowly.
   b. playing with rocks and sand in the sea.
   c. opening and closing their mouths.

 Score _____

Extra Practice

Circle True or False for each sentence.

1. A dolphin can swim.   True   False
2. Only people use language.   True   False
3. Scientists have studied dolphins.   True   False
4. Body language uses words.   True   False
5. Some animals are smart.   True   False

Levels in Nature

Animals get energy from the things that they eat. Some animals eat plants. Some eat other animals. Some eat plants and other animals. By looking at what eats what, we can learn how energy moves from one living thing to another.

One way to look at how energy moves from animal to animal is to imagine three
5 levels in nature. At the first level, plants and trees make their own food. Animals and insects are usually in the second level. These are living things that eat things from the first level. Sometimes, they eat things from the second level, too. Some animals eat plants, and then another big animal eats them. Very small animals that you can't even see are part of the third level. After a living thing dies, these very small animals break down its body.

10 We can imagine something like these three levels in the ocean, too. Some kinds of small sea life use the sunlight to make food. Then another kind of small sea life eats them. A
15 fish then eats the small sea life, and something larger eats the small fish. So energy moves between animals in the ocean just like it moves on land.

Word Count   200 words

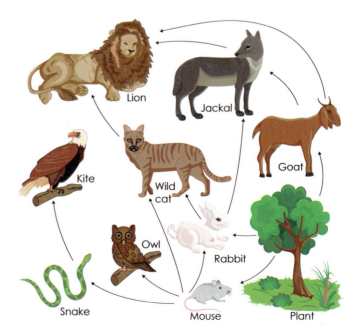

Comprehension Questions

Circle the right answer.

1. This reading is about
   a. things to eat in the ocean.
   b. how energy moves in nature.
   c. which animals eat plants.

2. Which of the following is true of the first level?
   a. The animals there have very little energy.
   b. All animals there are very small.
   c. Things there make their own food.

3. The writer says that animals and insects
   a. are found in the first level.
   b. are found in the second level.
   c. are found in the third level.

4. In the third level, very small animals
   a. eat only one kind of small sea animal.
   b. need sunlight to make the food they eat.
   c. break down the bodies of animals that die.

5. The writer says that in the ocean, energy moves
   a. more slowly than it does on land.
   b. in the same way as it does on land.
   c. from large animals to small animals.

 Score _____

Extra Practice

Circle the right word.

We can study how 1. (energy / life) moves in nature by looking at what eats what. An easy way to look at this is to 2. (imagine / learn) three levels in nature. The first level has things that make their own food in it. The second level has 3. (insects / scientists) and animals that eat things in the first and second levels. The third 4. (food / level) has very small animals that break down the bodies of things after they die. These three levels are the same in the 5. (ocean / plants) as they are on land.

A Dangerous Wind

In some parts of the world, when dark clouds fill the sky, a great danger sometimes appears. This danger is a quickly turning tower of air called a tornado, and it is one of the most dangerous things in nature.

Tornadoes happen mostly in the US, and they usually
5   form in the summer when warm, wet air and cold, dry
air meet. They appear at the bottom of large, dark
clouds. The wind under the cloud begins to go around
and around. It gets faster and faster and can become very
strong and dangerous. When the wind touches the ground,
10 it is called a tornado. The turning tornado moves along the
ground and can break down trees and buildings in its way.

Most tornadoes are small and only stay on the ground a
few minutes. However, even a small tornado can do a lot of damage.
Sometimes, tornadoes are very, very big and can last much longer. The
15 worst tornado ever traveled 352 km and was on the ground for three and a
half hours. Over 600 people died.

Tornadoes are so dangerous because they appear suddenly. There is often
no time to run and no place to hide from them.

Word Count   200 words

Comprehension Questions

Circle the right answer.

1. This reading is about
   a. dark clouds.
   b. rain storms.
   c. tornadoes.

2. Which of these is NOT needed to form a tornado?
   a. Rain
   b. Warm, wet air
   c. Cold, dry air

3. What does the wind in a tornado do?
   a. It goes in a straight line.
   b. It goes around and around.
   c. It goes up and down.

4. Tornadoes are so dangerous because
   a. they are always very big.
   b. they stay on the ground a long time.
   c. they appear suddenly.

5. How far did the worst tornado travel?
   a. About one kilometer
   b. Less than ten kilometers
   c. Over three hundred kilometers

 Score _____

Extra Practice

Circle True or False for each sentence.

1.	A tornado is made of quickly turning air.	True	False
2.	Tornadoes appear at the bottom of large dark clouds.	True	False
3.	In the worst tornado ever, 60 people died.	True	False
4.	Many tornadoes only stay on the ground for a few hours.	True	False
5.	Tornadoes are dangerous because they appear suddenly.	True	False

A Hard-Working Plant

Many people have Aloe vera plants in their homes. People have been growing Aloe vera for thousands of years. People used Aloe vera to help with health problems as long ago as 2100 BC.

Aloe vera is a plant that is usually found in hot, dry places. It has long, green
5   leaves, and it is a very hard-working plant. It can be used to help with cuts or burns. Aloe vera also cleans the air around it. Bad air can come from the paint on the walls of some houses. Aloe vera can make the air clean again. Aloe vera is also a good plant to have in your room at night when you sleep. It takes in the air you breathe out. The plant then gives off clean air that you breathe in.

10   Growing an Aloe vera plant at home is very easy! You can buy a plant at the store. Put it in a place where there is plenty of sunlight. Water your plant during the spring, summer, and fall. If
15   you want more Aloe vera plants, you can just break off part of the Aloe vera plant. You can put this in the ground to grow again.

Word Count   200 words

Time _____

Comprehension Questions

Circle the right answer.

1. This reading is about
    a. how Aloe vera works hard.
    b. how Aloe vera gives off bad air.
    c. how Aloe vera was used long ago.

2. Which of the following is NOT something that Aloe vera does?
    a. Gives off something bad like paint
    b. Gives off the air you breathe in
    c. Helps with health problems

3. People have been growing Aloe vera
    a. to use as a kind of paint.
    b. for thousands of years.
    c. as something to kill insects in their rooms.

4. You can grow more Aloe vera plants by
    a. giving special plant food to the Aloe vera plant.
    b. breaking off a part of the plant and planting it.
    c. giving the plant a lot of water.

5. The writer says that Aloe vera is good to have in your room because
    a. it will change colors to let you know you have a health problem.
    b. when you break off a part of the plant, it does not hurt the Aloe vera.
    c. it takes in the air you breathe out and gives off the air you breathe in.

 Score _____

Extra Practice

Circle the right word.

People like to grow Aloe vera plants in their homes. One thing that these plants are good for is your 1. (health / touch). You can use these plants to help with cuts or 2. (burns / walls). Aloe vera are also good because they clean the air you 3. (breathe / dry). These plants are easy to grow. Just put a piece of the plant in the ground in a place where it can get 4. (clouds / plenty) of sunlight. Give it water in the 5. (spring / wind), summer, and fall, and it will grow well!

Lost Forever?

People live all over the world. But they are not always very careful about how they live. People can cut down too many trees or put bad things into the water. This can hurt the plants, trees, and animals that live there. Sometimes, one kind of animal or tree dies out and is gone forever. But not all of these animals or trees are
5 gone forever. Some seem to be gone and then suddenly they come back!

This can happen to animals, plants, or trees. For a long time we think that they are gone. Since they are not seen for a long time, scientists say they have died out. Then someone finds one—or many! Scientists once said that one type of bird that could not fly was no longer living anywhere in the world. Then, in 2013, someone
10 saw one! The bird that could not fly was still there. This was good news. It shows us that there are many things we do not know about our world. It also shows us that we need to be careful about how we live. We need to take care of our world so that living things are not gone forever.

Word Count 200 words

Time

Circle the right answer.

1. This reading is about

    a. animals and plants that seem to be gone and then come back.

    b. plants and animals that are gone forever, and people like that.

    c. scientists who seem to have discovered new animals in nature.

2. What does the writer say about animals that are gone forever?

    a. Not all of the animals are really gone forever.

    b. There is more room for people because they are gone.

    c. Other animals must change once an animal is gone.

3. The writer says that

    a. people should put good things in the water.

    b. people should find more animals near cities.

    c. people should take care of the world around them.

4. At one time, scientists thought that

    a. birds made one kind of tree die out.

    b. a bird that could not fly was no more.

    c. when animals suddenly come back, it is bad news.

5. The writer says that people sometimes hurt

    a. the animals living in people's homes.

    b. only large animals, but not small animals.

    c. both plants and animals.

 Score _____

Extra Practice

Circle True or False for each sentence.

1.	People are always careful how they live.	True	False
2.	Scientists say something has died out if no one sees it for a week.	True	False
3.	Sometimes one kind plant or animal dies out and is gone forever.	True	False
4.	Sometimes one kind of plant or animal seems to be gone, but it isn't.	True	False
5.	A type of bird that was thought all gone was seen in 2013.	True	False

Chapter 2 · Music

A Look at the pictures. Write the right words.

advertisement	CD	computer	people
pipes	record	toys	video

Things that can make music:

1. _____

some 2. _____

a 3. _____

4. _____

When you might hear music:

in a(n) 5. _____

watching a(n) 6. _____

on a(n) 7. _____

playing a(n) 8. _____

B Write the right word in each blank.

advertisement	beans	affect	exciting	pain
pipe	pizza	records	reason	videos

1. Most people today listen to music through _____, not through CDs or _____.

2. One _____ my grandfather takes medicine every day is for the _____ in his legs.

3. Someone might order extra cheese on top of their _____, but never _____!

4. The size of the _____ will _____ the sound that it makes when you hit it.

5. We enjoyed watching the _____ TV _____, but we still don't know what it was advertising.

C Survey your classmates. Write the name of one person who. . .

1. . . . can sing an advertisement from radio or TV.   _____

2. . . . listens to music when exercising or working out.   _____

3. . . . has CDs with music on them at home.   _____

4. . . . watched an exciting band play live on stage.   _____

5. . . . was so affected by a song that it made him/her cry.   _____

D Complete the chart with words from the box.

computer	record	exciting	reason	shake	advertisement

Noun	Verb	Adjective
1.	record	recorded
excitement	excite	2.
3.	compute	computed
4.	advertise	advertised
shaker	5.	shaken
6.	reason	reasonable

Fun and Games and Music

Some people may not like video games. But they might like the music from some games! The pictures and story are a big part of why most people like video games. The music helps tell the game's story.

The first video games had simple sounds or music. However, computers became
5 faster and better. The music also got better. The sounds in a game are now very important. They help you feel like a part of the story.

A lot of music in the games makes you have a special feeling. Many times, the music is exciting. This happens when you win the game or get more points. But it can also be very soft, or it can make you feel afraid. Much of the music is played very well. This is a big
10 reason why people who usually do not like video games do like some of them: it's because of the music. They enjoy the sound of the nice music.

You can buy a CD with video game music on it to listen to at home or in the car. You do not have to be in front of a computer to enjoy the sounds of your favorite game!

Word Count 200 words

Time _____

Comprehension Questions

Circle the right answer.

1. This reading is about
   a. how the pictures and music in games tell a story.
   b. why the music in video games is scary.
   c. why people like the music from video games.

2. Most people like video games for
   a. the story and the pictures.
   b. the exciting fights in them.
   c. the money they win with them.

3. The music in games got better because
   a. computers got faster and better.
   b. the pictures and the stories changed.
   c. it makes you feel like you are really there.

4. Which of the following is NOT mentioned to describe video game music?
   a. Exciting
   b. Soft
   c. Dark

5. The writer says that people now listen to video game music
   a. with big, loud computers.
   b. in cars or other places.
   c. when they need energy.

 Score _____

Extra Practice

Circle the right word.

When you play a video game, the pictures and story of the game might seem most important. But the music used in the game can be another 1. (part / reason) for people to like the game. Video game music might be 2. (enjoying / exciting) in some parts of the game. It might be soft, or it might make players 3. (afraid / simple) in other parts of the game. Today, some video game music is so good that it has even been put on 4. (CDs / sounds). Then people can listen to the 5. (music / points) even when they aren't playing the game!

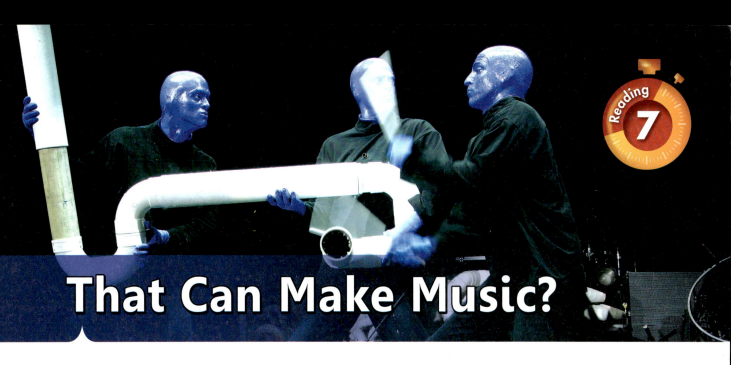

That Can Make Music?

There are many ways of making music in the world. You can use almost anything that will make a sound, even a piece of fruit! Some people on YouTube use food and a computer to make music. They can play music with different kinds of fruit.

5　　It is not just people with computers and food who can make music. The Blue Man Group uses everyday things to tell a story with their music. The group has become famous for their music shows. In their shows, the group uses a really long pipe. They move it around to make music. It is so big that two people in the group need to hold

10　it. The group also makes music by moving a long stick up and down and side to side.

A lot of people use different things to play music, such as food, computers, and water. You can also make music at home. Do you have a cup? You can put dry beans into

15　the cup and shake it. Even a glass of water can help you make music. The music comes from the way the players move and shake the different things. What can you use to make music?

Word Count　200 words

Time _____

Comprehension Questions

Circle the right answer.

1. This reading is about
   a. the Blue Man Group.
   b. making music with food.
   c. using things to make music.

2. The writer says that
   a. not many things can be used to make music.
   b. you can use almost anything to make music.
   c. you can use the music from the Blue Man Group.

3. The writer says that some people use a computer and
   a. a long pipe to make music.
   b. fruit to make music.
   c. cups made from pipes to make music.

4. The Blue Man Group makes music with
   a. a whole watermelon.
   b. a long pipe.
   c. a computer.

5. Which of the following is NOT mentioned as a thing that can make music?
   a. A bowl with jam in it
   b. A cup with beans in it
   c. A glass with water in it

 Score _____

Extra Practice

Circle True or False for each sentence.

1.	Even a piece of fruit can be used to make music.	True	False
2.	Only one person on YouTube uses food to make music.	True	False
3.	The Blue Man Group is famous for their video game.	True	False
4.	The Blue Man Group uses pipes and sticks to make music.	True	False
5.	You can shake dry beans in a cup to make music at home.	True	False

Healthy to Hear

Music affects the way we feel. When listening to music that they like, people work more happily. The way we feel can also affect our health. Let's look at some of the ways music does this.

Runners will run faster when there is fast music playing. They will also run
5 farther. Music even helps them after they stop running.

Doctors who work with people who are feeling a lot of pain sometimes use music to help them. If they are enjoying music, the pain seems to be less.

Some types of music can help people to sleep. When
10 people cannot sleep well, it can affect their lives in bad ways. Sometimes they take things to help them sleep. But too much of this can hurt them. Music never hurts, and it does not cost anything!

Music can also help us think more clearly. One study
15 showed that people did better on tests when they were listening to music. A later study showed that test-takers only did better if they really liked the music.

If you want to get more out of your work and your running, feel less pain, sleep better, or do
20 better on tests, music can help.

Word Count 200 words

 Time _____

Comprehension Questions

Circle the right answer.

1. This reading is about
   a. why unhealthy people should listen to music.
   b. how music is used to treat very sick people.
   c. the effect of music on different areas of life.

2. What is NOT a way music improves a runner's workout?
   a. By motivating the runner to run faster
   b. By helping the runner breathe
   c. By making the runner run longer

3. What is a way in which doctors use music?
   a. To help sick people feel less pain
   b. To make sick people feel like exercising
   c. To create a good environment

4. What does the writer say about listening to music while taking a test?
   a. The right music can help test-takers.
   b. Test-takers do better when it is quiet.
   c. Teachers enjoy listening to music while students take tests.

5. Which of the following can be said about music?
   a. Music can make people want to change their life.
   b. Slow music is better for our health than fast music.
   c. Music can help us exercise, sleep, and think.

 Score _____

Extra Practice

Circle the right word.

People have found that music can 1. (affect / shake) our health. Runners use music to help them run faster and 2. (bigger / farther). Doctors may play music in the hospital to help people feel 3. (less / simple) pain. People who can't sleep can listen to music and fall asleep. Then they don't have to take things that may 4. (hurt / win) them over time. Music never hurts, and it doesn't cost money every time you listen to it. Even students have found that listening to music can help them think more 5. (softly / clearly) when studying.

Music That Stays in Your Head

Have you ever had a song which stays in your head? Have you ever heard a song that made you feel good? Music can do this very well. And people who make advertisements know this. They use music in TV and radio advertisements. It makes the advertisements work better.

5   When companies make advertisements, they want people to remember them. A good song can make that happen. You might hear an advertisement for a pizza place. The phone number is put to music. Two weeks later, when you want pizza, it is easy to remember the phone number. Because it was put to music, you remember it.

10   Sometimes, advertisements work just because the song makes you feel good. You are not sure why, but when you are at the store and you see the thing, you feel happy. So you buy it. Music is selling it to you.

Sometimes, the writers of advertisements use music to tell you a story. The words of the advertisement can tell people 15 why they should buy something. The words give people a reason to buy. But the music makes it more interesting. Because the music makes people listen, the words get through. Music sells!

Word Count   200 words

 Time

Comprehension Questions

Circle the right answer.

1. This reading is about
   a. how to make a popular pizza restaurant.
   b. how music can be used in advertisements.
   c. how music can trick people into buying things.

2. Why do companies use music in advertising?
   a. It is a cheap way to get people to try new things.
   b. It can make advertisements work better.
   c. It scares people into buying things.

3. What is NOT a reason music works well?
   a. It can help people to remember things.
   b. People connect feelings with products.
   c. Famous people will get their fans to buy things.

4. What part of an advertisement with music is used to give information?
   a. How fast or slow the song is
   b. How high or low the song is
   c. What the singer says

5. What does the writer think about the use of music in advertising?
   a. It causes information to get lost.
   b. It may make some advertisements too long.
   c. It is a good way to sell things.

 Score _____

Extra Practice

Circle True or False for each sentence.

1.	Music is used in TV and radio advertisements.	True	False
2.	A good song can make people remember an advertisement.	True	False
3.	A phone number put to music is easy to remember.	True	False
4.	A good advertisement song can make people feel pain.	True	False
5.	The words of a song should give people a reason not to buy something.	True	False

Only Voices

Pentatonix is a group known for their singing. They make music with only their voices! Pentatonix started with three friends. The three friends liked to sing together when they were

5   students. Then two more people joined the group. Each person sings a different part of the music.

The singers named their group Pentatonix. This name comes from five notes used in music. The singers like

10 this name because their group has five people in it. Today, Pentatonix is famous, but they almost did not get to sing!

Pentatonix sang on a special music show in 2011. There were many other groups on the show. They all really wanted to win. But Pentatonix won! The group got $200,000. They also got a chance to sing music for a company. But the company

15 did not let Pentatonix sing, because they thought that the group was not good enough. But Pentatonix kept on trying. They put their songs on the internet. People loved their music and bought it! One of their records became the best-selling Christmas record since 1962!

After that, Pentatonix sang in a movie. The group is still singing today. They

20 now go all over the world to sing their music.

Word Count   200 words

 Time _____

Comprehension Questions

Circle the right answer.

1. This reading is about

    a. five people who started a singing show.

    b. how a group of singers did not give up.

    c. why people like to watch Pentatonix on TV.

2. Which of the following is NOT mentioned about the group's name?

    a. It is related to five notes in music.

    b. It is related to the number of people in the group.

    c. It is also the name of their famous Christmas record.

3. Pentatonix won on the show and

    a. got $200,000 and a chance to sing more music.

    b. then worked on the show to choose the next winners.

    c. made a TV advertisement about their Christmas record.

4. Pentatonix did not give up, but instead they

    a. sang their songs on a show.

    b. put their songs on the internet.

    c. started to make movies.

5. The writer says that Pentatonix

    a. made movies about Christmas.

    b. were in a movie and are now traveling.

    c. were sad because their music did not win.

 Score _____

Extra Practice

Circle the right word.

The group called Pentatonix makes music with only their 1. (notes / voices). The first people in the group were friends, but then two more 2. (bought / joined) the group. When the group started, they almost did not get a chance to sing. Pentatonix won on a 3. (music / pizza) show, but a company thought they were not good enough. The group put their 4. (name / songs) on the internet, and people loved them. One of their 5. (records / types) became the best-selling Christmas record in fifty years!

Chapter 3 Health

A Look at the pictures. Write the right words.

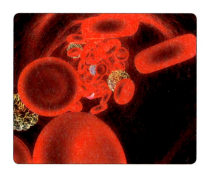

1. _____

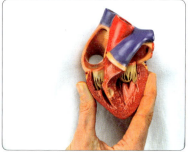

2. _____

3. _____

exercise   heart   healthy

hospital   blood cells   vitamins

4. _____

5. _____

6. _____

B **Which sentences are true? Put a check (✓) in the box.**

1. You can get vitamins by eating fruits and vegetables. ☐

2. Hamburgers and French fries are not healthy foods. ☐

3. A person's heart has bones in it. ☐

4. Stress makes many people feel calm and relaxed. ☐

5. There may be areas with no hospitals far from big cities. ☐

C **Work with a classmate. Ask your classmate the questions below and write his/her answers. Then share the answers with a different classmate.**

1. What helps you calm down or handle stress? _____

2. Have you stayed in a hospital? If so, why? _____

3. Who in your family has broken a bone? _____

4. If you need more vitamin C, what can you eat or drink? _____

5. What is a healthy heart rate for a man or woman? _____

D **Read the clues. Find the words in the box to complete the puzzle.**

area	calm	cell	healthy	heart	stress

1. When you have good health, you are ____.

2. This is a very small thing in blood.

3. When you are not excited, you are ____.

4. This is one part of a larger place.

5. When you are in trouble, you feel ____.

➡ The secret word: _____

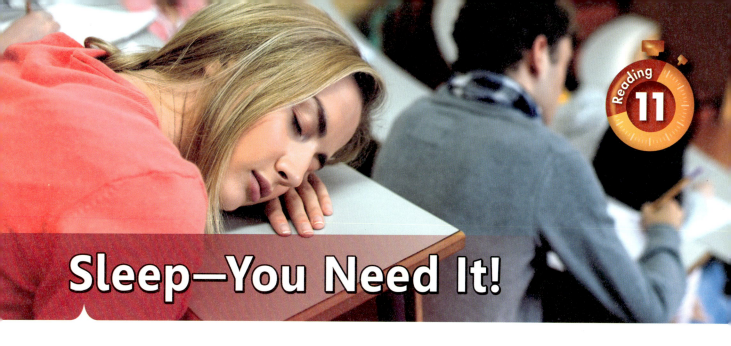

Sleep—You Need It!

Do we really need to sleep? While scientists do not understand everything about sleep, they do know it is very important. When you sleep, your body is not moving. But your mind is busy!

Sleep helps with many things. Sleep helps you remember what you learned during the day. It stores that learning for a long time. One study showed good effects for students who studied just before going to sleep. Sleeping slowed down the time that the students forgot things. Sleep also cleans out the bad things in your body. Your body gets hurt during the day when you run or play. The body fixes what is hurt when you sleep. Your body also grows while you are sleeping.

Everyone needs sleep. Men and women need 7 to 9 hours of sleep every night. Students need a lot of sleep, but they usually do not get enough. Students who are in high school need 8 to 10 hours of sleep every night. They need much more sleep than older people because they are still growing. They also need to learn a lot. The extra hours in bed help with this. Getting enough sleep is important for learning, growing, and remembering.

Word Count 200 words

Circle the right answer.

1. This reading is about
   a. why sleep is hard to get.
   b. why we need sleep.
   c. why adults need less sleep.

2. The writer says that
   a. scientists understand sleep well.
   b. scientists know sleep is important.
   c. scientists know the brain is busy.

3. If you want to remember a lot, you should
   a. keep busy but slow down.
   b. talk while you write things.
   c. study before sleeping.

4. Which of the following is NOT mentioned as a benefit of sleep?
   a. It helps you grow.
   b. It cleans your body.
   c. It makes you study.

5. The writer says that
   a. students do not sleep enough.
   b. adults sleep a lot.
   c. scientists do not sleep much.

 Score _____

Extra Practice

Circle True or False for each sentence.

1.	Scientists understand everything about sleep.	True	False
2.	When you sleep, your body and mind are not working.	True	False
3.	Sleeping seems to slow down the time students forget things.	True	False
4.	The body fixes what is hurt when you are sleeping.	True	False
5.	High school students need less sleep than older people.	True	False

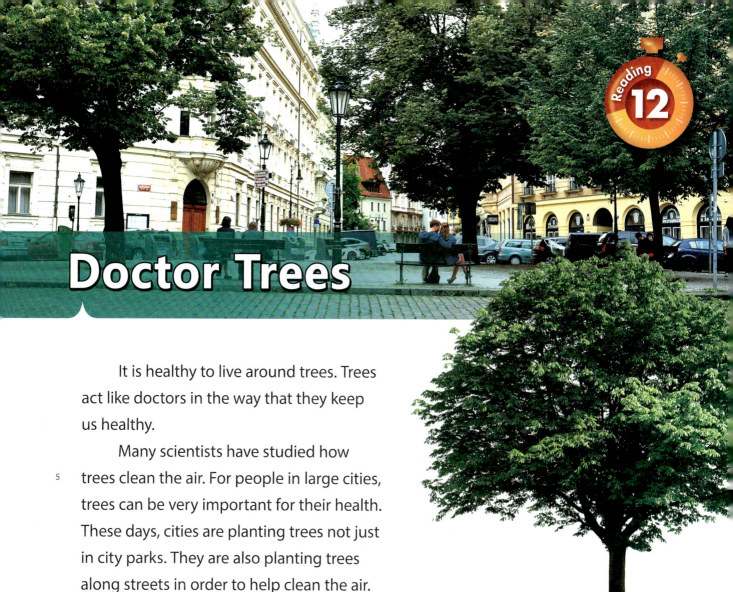

Doctor Trees

It is healthy to live around trees. Trees act like doctors in the way that they keep us healthy.

Many scientists have studied how
5 trees clean the air. For people in large cities, trees can be very important for their health. These days, cities are planting trees not just in city parks. They are also planting trees along streets in order to help clean the air.

10 Some scientists also believe trees help more than just the air. Trees keep our bodies healthy as well. People in hospitals seem to do better when they can see trees from their room. People with trees near their homes usually exercise more.

Scientists have also been studying the healthy effects of trees on our minds.
15 One effect of trees seems to be that they make people feel less stress. One study looked at city people in an area with few trees. After trees were planted on the street, people living there said the area was much nicer. They walked slower when going to work or to home. They stayed on the street to talk more often with people who lived near them.

20 Of course, another good effect is that doctor trees work for free!

Word Count 200 words

Time _____

Circle the right answer.

1. This reading is about
   a. how trees help our health.
   b. one kind of healthy tree.
   c. trees around hospitals.

2. The writer says that
   a. trees work faster than doctors.
   b. trees don't grow well in cities.
   c. trees help people in cities.

3. Which of the following is NOT mentioned as a benefit of trees?
   a. Calming people
   b. Cleaning the air
   c. Making places cooler

4. Where trees are found on streets, people seem to
   a. have more pets.
   b. meet more often.
   c. walk faster.

5. The writer says that people don't have to
   a. look at trees.
   b. pay trees.
   c. plant trees.

 Score _____

Extra Practice

Circle the right word.

Living around trees can keep us healthy because trees 1. (act / affect) like doctors! One thing that trees do for us is clean the 2. (air / city) we breathe. But scientists think that trees help us in more ways, too. When sick people are in the 3. (hospital / street), they seem to do better when they can see trees from their rooms. Trees also seem to make people feel less 4. (mind / stress). People like to walk or exercise in 5. (areas / effects) where there are more trees.

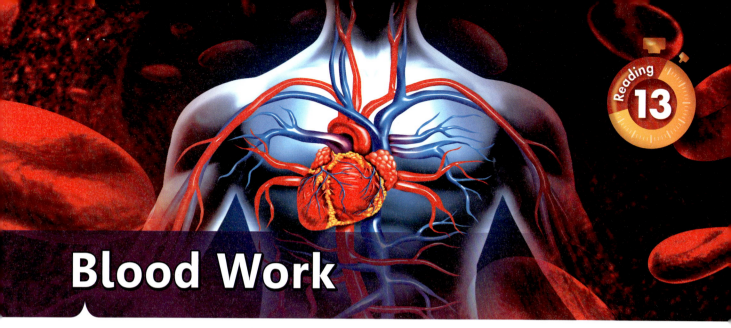

Blood Work

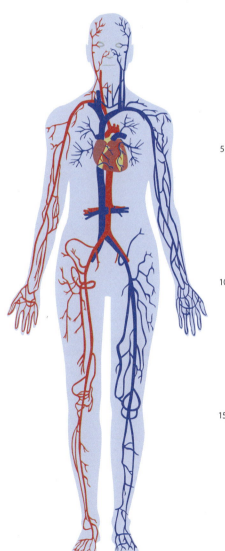

Your blood is very important to your health because your blood brings food to every part of your body. It also carries away the bad things from your body. That is why you must take care of your blood.

5   A man has about 5 liters of blood, and a child has about 2.5 liters of blood. This is about 7 to 8% of their body. Blood contains red and white cells. Red and white blood cells are made in the bones. Red blood cells make the blood red, and they live for about 120 days. White
10 blood cells fight bad things in the body. They only live for around 3 to 4 days.

    When you breathe in, the air goes into your body. In the body, the red blood cells take up the air, and this makes the blood red. It goes into the left side of your
15 heart. The heart moves this blood to the rest of your body. The blood gives the oxygen to all parts of your body and takes up bad things to get them out from your body. Then the blood comes back to the right side of the heart. This blood looks blue.

Word Count   200 words

 **Time** _____

Circle the right answer.

1. This reading is about
   a. blood and how it is used in hospitals.
   b. how blood moves and helps the body.
   c. the amount of blood in people who are not healthy.

2. A man has about 5 liters of blood in his body,
   a. which is about 7-8% of his weight.
   b. which is about 3-4% of the blood for a child.
   c. and that is all of the water in the body.

3. Which of the following is NOT mentioned about blood?
   a. What different kinds of cells there are
   b. The parts inside cells that need energy
   c. How long cells live inside the body

4. The writer says that blood
   a. is blue when a person is sick.
   b. is something hospitals need.
   c. is moved around by the heart.

5. Where does the red blood go?
   a. To all the white blood cells
   b. To the right side of the lungs
   c. To the left side of the heart

 Score _____

Extra Practice

Circle True or False for each sentence.

1.	Red blood cells are made in bones.	True	False
2.	Blood carries away bad things from parts of your body.	True	False
3.	A child has more than 5 liters of blood.	True	False
4.	Blood contains red and yellow cells.	True	False
5.	The air that you breathe in makes your blood turn blue.	True	False

Are You Under Stress?

Everyone feels stress sometimes. You feel stress when you have a lot of work to do and not enough time. You can also feel stress when you have problems. Sometimes, a little stress can be good. But usually, stress is bad.

Too much stress can cause health problems. Stress can make it hard to sleep
5 well. It can also make it difficult to finish school work. If you have a health problem, stress can make it worse.

There are some things you can do to feel less stress. You can talk to your parents or a friend about your feelings. Talking about stress can help you understand it. How can you take away the
10 problem that is making you feel stress? Sometimes, writing down the problem and writing ways to take it away can help.

Exercise is also a good way to help with stress. Different exercises, like playing sports or walking, can help you feel better. Make sure that you are taking care of
15 yourself. Getting enough sleep, eating the right kinds of food, and having time to sit still are all important.

If you feel that you have too much stress, tell other people and get some help.

Word Count 200 words

Circle the right answer.

1. This reading is about
   a. how to feel more stress.
   b. stress and how to handle it.
   c. the ways that people feel stress.

2. Sometimes stress can be good, but
   a. it can affect beauty.
   b. it can also be very bad.
   c. it is always easy to handle.

3. Which of the following is NOT mentioned as a way to handle stress?
   a. Playing sports
   b. Talking to someone
   c. Doing school work

4. The writer says that if you cannot handle your stress, you should
   a. ask for help.
   b. make a plan.
   c. exercise.

5. Stress can cause you
   a. to lose sleep and exercise more.
   b. to talk to other people and study.
   c. to lose sleep and have health problems.

 Score _____

Extra Practice

Circle the right word.

Things like too much work or 1. (parents / problems) in life can make us feel stress. A little stress can be good for us, but too much 2. (stress / time) can cause health problems. When you have too much stress, you may not be able to 3. (fight / finish) work for school. You may not be able to sleep well. Stress can also make small health problems become 4. (better / worse). Some ways to help you feel less stress are talking to others about your stress, 5. (containing / exercising), and writing things down.

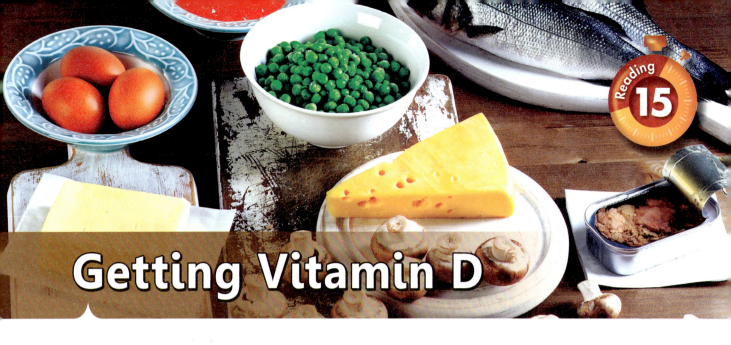

Getting Vitamin D

Around 80 percent of people do not get enough vitamin D every day. But this vitamin is very important for your health.

Vitamin D is really important for our bones. When we are young, vitamin D builds up our bones and makes them strong. When we are older, we still need
5 vitamin D to keep our bones strong. Our bodies keep the vitamin D that we take in inside our bones and teeth. Then we lose vitamin D as we work and exercise during the day. But our bodies can't make vitamin D. We have to get it from outside of our bodies.

So where can a person get this very important vitamin? Vitamin D is in foods
10 like fish and eggs. Sometimes, vitamin D is added to bread, milk, and orange juice.

Food is not the only way our bodies can get vitamin D. The sun also gives us vitamin D. If we want to be healthy, we should spend some time in the sun each day. Too much sun is not good for you, but around 15 minutes a day is usually enough. And we should be sure to eat foods that are rich in vitamin D, too.

Word Count   200 words

⏱ Time _____

Comprehension Questions

Circle the right answer.

1. This reading is about
   a. how much vitamin D we need.
   b. where we get vitamin D from.
   c. why people don't like vitamin D.

2. The writer says that this vitamin
   a. is found in foods cooked with bones.
   b. is made inside people's bones.
   c. is needed for good bones.

3. Which of the following is NOT mentioned about vitamin D?
   a. What the "D" means
   b. Where we get it
   c. Why we need it

4. Some good foods to eat that naturally have this vitamin are
   a. any green foods.
   b. fish and eggs.
   c. milk and orange juice

5. The writer says that people can also get this vitamin
   a. from red blood cells.
   b. from going outside.
   c. from pills or medicine.

 Score _____

Extra Practice

Circle True or False for each sentence.

1. Around 8 percent of people do not get enough vitamin D.   True   False
2. Vitamin D is not very important for our bones.   True   False
3. Our bodies keep vitamin D inside our bones and teeth.   True   False
4. Our bodies make vitamin D when we exercise.   True   False
5. Foods like fish and eggs have vitamin D in them.   True   False

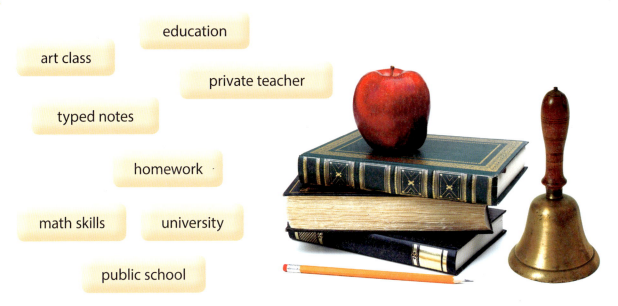

Chapter 4 Education

A **Which of the following are places of learning? Circle the words.**

education

art class

private teacher

typed notes

homework

math skills   university

public school

B **Draw lines to make correct sentences.**

1. Doing homework is • • a big part of • • math teacher.

2. I suggest that you • • schools do not teach • • one's education.

3. I don't write by hand • • very quickly, so I • • the subject of art.

4. Some public • • look for a private • • to study in university.

5. You can choose • • some subjects you want • • usually type my notes.

C Work in groups with your classmates. Can you think of examples for all of these ideas related to education? Share your examples with the class.

| The name of an expensive private university: | Subjects that only some students study in public high schools: | Homework that must be typed: | A song in another language that you know some words of: |

D Fill in the puzzle with words from the box.

art	education	homework	math	private
probably	skilled	song	subject	suggest

Across

2. what you get from school
4. one thing to study in school
5. very likely; there is a good chance that
9. to give a good idea to someone

Down

1. work you have to do for class
3. being good at something
5. not public
6. painting, drawing, etc.
7. what you sing
8. the subject where you study numbers

Art in the Classroom

What should teachers spend time teaching? Many say that math and reading are the most important things. And if students are not doing well, the teacher should spend more time on those subjects. These students should spend less time on the arts, they say.

But studies show that studying art is important. It does more than help students
5   draw and paint and sing. In fact, it helps them in math and reading and science. Students who study art are better learners. They are better thinkers and speakers. They are also better at working with people and understanding their feelings.

In addition, art makes learning more fun. It makes students want to learn. It makes it easier to keep thinking about one thing. More and more
10   students today seem to have trouble doing that! Students also feel good about themselves when art is part of their work. They learn to see the world in a new way, and that is good for every part of their lives.

Schools that stop teaching art are making a
15   mistake. That is not the way to make students better at math and reading. More and better art classes are the best way to do that.

Word Count   200 words

Time

Comprehension Questions

Circle the right answer.

1. This reading is about
    a. the benefits of studying art.
    b. how art is just as important as math.
    c. how art is becoming less popular.

2. What is NOT something that gets better or higher by studying art?
    a. Students' thinking
    b. Students' speaking
    c. Students' level of stress

3. What is mentioned as something art helps students to do?
    a. Sleep better at night
    b. Keep working on one thing
    c. Get into university

4. What, according to the writer, is the main reason to teach art in school?
    a. To benefit the minds of young people
    b. To give the world more beauty through art
    c. To help students' math scores

5. What does the writer think is the best way to get better math and reading scores?
    a. More colorful books to study
    b. Keep art classes in schools
    c. Give students more time to study

 Score _____

Extra Practice

Circle the right word.

Many people think that 1. (math / music) and reading are the most important things to learn in school. If students are not doing well in these 2. (speakers / subjects), people think teachers need to spend more time on them. Less time can be spent on subjects like 3. (art / fun) because they are not important. But thinking that way may be a 4. (mistake / part). Studies show that subjects like art can actually help students do better in math, reading, and 5. (songs / science).

Does Homework Help?

Should students have to do extra school work at home? Some people say it is important. Others say homework hurts students more than it helps them.

People who think homework is important say students who work more learn more. Homework helps students remember things. And it is important to learn how

5 to work independently. There is not enough time, they say, to learn everything in class. Students must do more at home. Only at home do students have the time to really think about what they are learning.

But homework can be a problem. Students see learning as work. They do not enjoy it. And it takes up their time. They are in school all day as it is. When

10 homework is added, they have less time to interact with their families and friends. Play is important for a child's health.

The answer is probably somewhere in the middle. Teachers should not give homework just so that students will have to work more. But some work can be done outside of class.

15 Students can work on new skills that they might not get at school. As long as the work is interesting, students will not think it is so bad.

Word Count 200 words

 Time _____

Comprehension Questions

Circle the right answer.

1. This reading is about
    a. why students should not get homework.
    b. how parents should help children in their studies.
    c. if extra work for students is important or not.

2. Which is NOT mentioned as a reason to give homework?
    a. To help students' memory
    b. To work independently
    c. To get parents to help

3. Which of the following is mentioned as a problem with homework?
    a. It is impossible for students to have jobs.
    b. Students have little free time for family and play.
    c. Young people get less sleep than they need.

4. What should teachers think about when giving homework?
    a. If they will need to check it
    b. If the work is too difficult
    c. If the students have time

5. What does the writer think about homework?
    a. Parents need to help their children with it more often.
    b. It is OK sometimes, but only if it is useful.
    c. It should not be given at all in high schools.

 Score _____

Extra Practice

Circle True or False for each sentence.

1. Everyone says that extra homework is important.   True   False
2. When students do work at home, they have more time to think about it.   True   False
3. Homework time can take away time with family and friends.   True   False
4. It is probably good for students to do some work outside of class.   True   False
5. Even interesting homework should not be given to students.   True   False

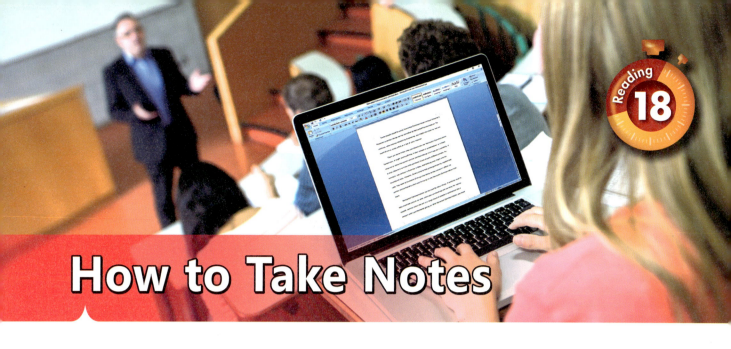

How to Take Notes

Taking notes is an important part of learning. Students listen to the teacher. They write down the important things. Or they use a computer. These days, many students take a computer to class to type their notes.

Some people think that using a computer is better. People type faster than
5 they write. That means they can write more. If you can type fast, you can type every word the teacher says.

Computers are becoming very common in classrooms. Almost every student in university has a computer small enough to take to class in order to type their notes. Fewer students write things down. Thus, there is a trend in schools now to focus
10 less on teaching kids how to write. Schools are moving away from teaching younger students how to write by hand. Many people see no need for writing by hand.

However, studies suggest that it is good to write things down. When a person can't write every word, they have to think about it more. They have
15 to pick out what is important. And the act of writing seems to help the person to remember. Studies show that people who write down their notes remember the information better.

Word Count 200 words

Time _____

Circle the right answer.

1. This reading is about
   a. typing vs. computers.
   b. listening vs. writing by hand.
   c. writing by hand vs. typing.

2. Which way of taking notes allows students to record more information?
   a. Typing
   b. Studying
   c. Writing by hand

3. Which way of taking notes helps students to remember more information?
   a. Typing
   b. Talking
   c. Writing by hand

4. What are some teachers doing because more students are using computers?
   a. Teaching students how to type
   b. Focusing more on writing clearly by hand
   c. Not teaching writing by hand in lessons

5. What do studies suggest about note-taking?
   a. Students should take notes by hand.
   b. Students should take notes by recording the class.
   c. Students should take notes by typing them.

 Score _____

Extra Practice

Circle the right word.

Students who take a computer to class are able to 1. (miss / type) important things they hear. Students who type very fast can take notes on 2. (almost / already) everything the teacher says. In 3. (middle / university) classes, it is easy to see students with computers for taking notes. With more and more students typing, teachers are spending 4. (fewer / less) time teaching writing skills. But writing by hand may be better for students because they 5. (seem / suggest) to remember things better that way.

A Part of Learning

Mothers often sing to their babies. It helps them get to know each other. And it teaches the baby language. Hearing the same words again and again is good for learning language.

5　This is true for second languages, too. Students and teachers get to know each other through music. Music is fun. When people have fun together, they become friends. Music also repeats a lot. Songs have words that rhyme. These things help memory. People can listen to a song many times. Soon, they will know the

10　words.

But meaning is important. It won't help you to learn the words of a song if you don't know what they mean. A class can talk about the song. If it is about something interesting, students will learn the meaning.

15　Music is also great for dancing. Many teachers find that when students move around, they learn better. It is important for students to get up out of their seats. When we use language, we are not always sitting. We use language when we move around. So we should learn language when we are moving, too.

20　Music is a big part of life. It should also be a big part of language learning.

Word Count　200 words

Comprehension Questions

Circle the right answer.

1. This reading is about
   a. an idea for learning language.
   b. how one's first language is learned.
   c. songs in two languages.

2. Why, according to the writer, do mothers sing to their babies?
   a. To grow closer to them and to teach
   b. To put them to sleep quickly
   c. To feel less stress as a parent

3. What is said to be a way that songs help learning?
   a. Hearing a song with a drum helps to know the meaning of words.
   b. Hearing the same words again and again helps memory.
   c. Hearing many people sing together helps students enjoy the lesson.

4. What, according to the writer, are two important things when it comes to learning?
   a. Working hard and being clear
   b. Having fun and remembering
   c. Moving a lot for exercise and health

5. What is NOT said to be an activity that can go along with a song?
   a. A discussion
   b. A dance
   c. A quiz

 Score _____

Extra Practice

Circle True or False for each sentence.

1. Mothers can teach their babies language by singing to them.   True   False
2. Music can help students learn a second language.   True   False
3. Songs with lots of different words are best for language learning.   True   False
4. Students should learn the meaning of songs when they study them.   True   False
5. Students learn best when they just sit in their seats and listen.   True   False

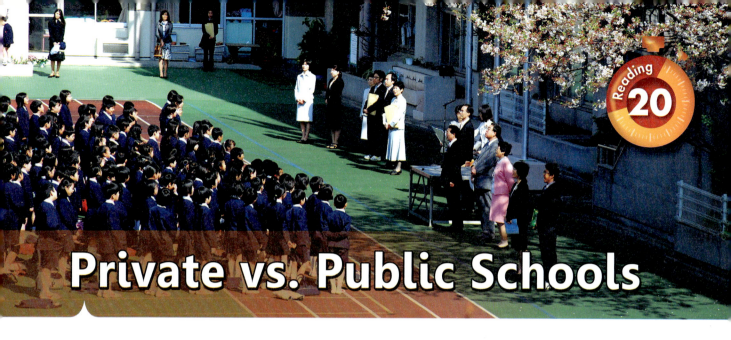

Private vs. Public Schools

All parents want their kids to get a good education. But are private schools or public schools better for that?

A lot of people think that because private school is expensive, it must be better. And as it turns out, students who go to private schools do better on tests. And they go to university more often.

But why is that? Is it because the education is better? Or is it because of who the students are? First, you have to be a good student to go to private school. Also, students who go to private schools come from rich families. They have more books. They probably have smartphones and a computer at home. These are the things that help students do better. Kids in public schools who have a home life like this also do well.

There is one thing that students at public school get that private school students do not. They spend time interacting with people who are not just like them. That is an important part of education, too. Tests are one thing. But children need to learn how to live in the world. Being with all kinds of people is one way to learn that.

Word Count 200 words

Time _____

Circle the right answer.

1. This reading is about
    a. why people are sending their kids to private schools.
    b. good things about different kinds of schools.
    c. how public schools teach kids without much money.

2. Who, according to the passage, performs better on tests as a group?
    a. Private school students
    b. Public school students
    c. They perform the same.

3. What is NOT listed as something affecting how students perform in schools?
    a. The books that students can read
    b. The kinds of teachers that students learn from
    c. The computers that students can use

4. Why do more private school students go to university?
    a. Because they receive better tests
    b. Because of their home life
    c. Because they have better life skills

5. What does the writer think is good about the education received at public schools?
    a. Better books and computers
    b. Clear goals of education at every grade level
    c. Many different kinds of classmates

 Score _____

Extra Practice

Circle the right word.

> Parents can choose to send their children to private schools or public schools for an 1. (education / idea). Is one better than the other? Private schools can be 2. (expensive / extra), but students in such schools do better on tests and often go to university. Maybe this is because the students come from 3. (area / rich) families, not because the schools are better. Such families have computers and lots of books in their homes. 4. (Public / World) school kids who are from homes like this also do well on tests and go to 5. (studies / university).

A Look at the pictures. Circle the right words.

1. This man knows a lot about (business / the law).

2. The company's (brand / desk) is known by millions of people.

3. This (restaurant / trust) is known for its homemade bread.

4. On my birthday, my mom made a cake and poured lemon sauce over the (expensive / whole) thing!

B Check (✓) the right answer.

1. What do you hear at most birthday parties?
   ☐ The birthday song   ☐ A strange law

2. Where would one usually have a business meeting?
   ☐ In an office   ☐ On a street

3. What do all businesses work hard to advertise?
   ☐ Their brand   ☐ Their toys

4. Why do people like to buy brand name clothes?
   ☐ They are expensive.   ☐ They look nice.

5. What is normal to find in millions of offices?
   ☐ Desks   ☐ Gardens

C Work with a group of classmates. Ask each other these questions.

1. What is the most expensive restaurant you have eaten at?

2. What is one toy that you received as a birthday present?

3. What is a brand that you trust to make good snacks?

4. What does your father or mother usually do after spending the whole day at work?

5. Do you know any small business owners? What kind of business do they have?

D Look at each group of words. Circle the word that does not belong in each group. Why doesn't it belong?

1. believe in	count on	trust in	work on
2. all	broken	complete	whole
3. chair	desk	table	window
4. birthday party	hospital	restaurant	toy store
5. expensive	important	special	tired

Proper Nouns to Know

Study these words that you will find in the readings for this chapter.

| Coca-Cola | McDonald's | September | Summy |

A Job for Everyone?

As kids get older, they need money. They need money for lunch and fun. They need money for toys and games. At first, a kid may only need a little money from time to time. But the things he or she needs get more expensive over time. At some point, the money from parents is not enough. Then it is time for that young person to get a job.

5   The first job that a person has is usually not the job he or she will keep all through life. Young people often change jobs before they find the jobs they want to keep. In the US, most people go through ten different jobs before they are forty years old!

10   With young people changing jobs so often, it is interesting that one kind of job stands out from the rest. There are more than 300 million people in the US. Imagine a group of ten of those people in the US. Of these ten

15   people, one or two of them have worked at the same restaurant, and that is true for every ten people in the US! What is the restaurant that has a job for almost everyone? It is McDonald's.

Word Count   200 words

Comprehension Questions

Circle the right answer.

1. This reading is about
   - a. a job that kids make.
   - b. jobs that people have.
   - c. the easiest job to have.

2. What is NOT mentioned as something that kids need money for?
   - a. Education
   - b. Food
   - c. Toys

3. What is mentioned about the first job that many people get?
   - a. It is not the job they stay at for life.
   - b. It is the job they usually keep for ten years.
   - c. It is the job they want again when they are forty.

4. According to the writer, how many times do people in the US change jobs before they turn forty?
   - a. Three times
   - b. Five times
   - c. Ten times

5. In which kind of place do many people in the US work at some point in their lives?
   - a. In a hospital
   - b. In a restaurant
   - c. In a school

 Score _____

Extra Practice

Circle True or False for each sentence.

1.	Kids buy more expensive things as they get older.	True	False
2.	People will probably keep their first jobs their whole lives.	True	False
3.	In the US, most people go through forty jobs before they are fifty.	True	False
4.	Many people in the US work for the same restaurant at some point in their lives.	True	False
5.	It is not easy for a person to get a job at McDonald's.	True	False

The Work Week

In school, were some days better than others for you? On your good days, maybe you learned the most from your classes. Or maybe you had the most energy to do things on those good days.

The same is true for people who work. Some days of work are better than others. When it comes to days in the office, the best days are the ones when the most work is done. From a study of offices and businesses, people found that Tuesday is the best day for work during the week.

That is not so surprising when you think about Monday, the first day of the working week. On Monday, a worker might be slower than usual because he or she had at least one day away from work. So the worker needs some time to get back to doing his or her best job. By Tuesday, a worker can be back to working as usual.

That does not mean, however, that Monday is the worst day of the week in the office. It was found that the least work is usually done on Fridays. Maybe that is because people become more tired by the end of the week.

Word Count   200 words

Time

Circle the right answer.

1. This reading is about
   a. how long people want to work in a week.
   b. how many days are in the work week.
   c. how much work is done on different days.

2. Which is NOT mentioned as a place where "good" and "bad" days are compared?
   a. At home
   b. At school
   c. At work

3. Which of the following is mentioned as the best day of the work week?
   a. Thursday
   b. Tuesday
   c. Friday

4. Why might less work get done on Monday?
   a. Because people use all of their energy to get to the office
   b. Because the least number of people work on Monday
   c. Because workers had at least one day off before that

5. On which day of the week is the least amount of work done?
   a. Monday
   b. Tuesday
   c. Friday

 Score _____

Extra Practice

Circle the right word.

For people in the 1. (business / student) world, some days are better than others. Maybe it is because people have more 2. (energy / rest) on some days than others. When people studied which days in the office were good and bad, some 3. (expensive / surprising) things were found. Most work gets done in 4. (offices / weeks) on Tuesdays. The worst day in the office is not Monday, though. The 5. (least / less) amount of work is done on Fridays.

Desks at the Office

People usually sit when they work. So people who work all day end up sitting for most of the day. But this is bad for a person's health. When we sit for too long every day, we don't move very much. So it is easy to start getting fat. Sitting too long is also bad for our work because it makes us want to sleep. When this happens,
5   people can make more mistakes in their work or take longer to finish work. Companies need workers to be healthy, so how do they fix the problem?

Some workplaces have different types of desks to help their workers. The first type of desk is the standing desk. The desk can be taller when a person wants to stand. It can also be shorter when the person wants to sit. Another type of desk is
10   the walking desk. This desk is made so that a person can work while walking at the same time.

Of course, no one can or should stand or walk while working for the whole day. After all, it would be very tiring. But these desks are useful if used for a short time and
15   several times a day.

Word Count 200 words

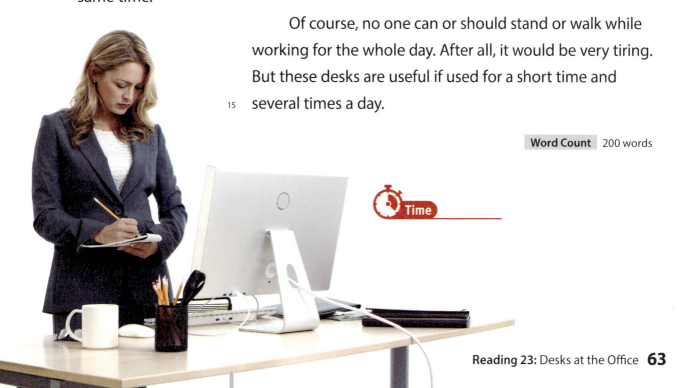

Time _____

Comprehension Questions

Circle the right answer.

1. This reading is about
   a. desks that help people work better.
   b. companies that have better workers.
   c. places to work that are fun.

2. The writer says that
   a. workers like to sit too much.
   b. sitting too long is bad.
   c. desks are too expensive.

3. Companies need workers to be
   a. sitting all day.
   b. healthy and hard-working.
   c. slow when working.

4. Which of the following is NOT mentioned as a type of desk that helps workers?
   a. A running desk
   b. A walking desk
   c. A standing desk

5. The writer says that it is good to use standing or walking desks
   a. for part of the work day, but not all day.
   b. all day at the office to stay healthy.
   c. on Friday when workers do the least work.

 Score _____

Extra Practice

Circle True or False for each sentence.

1.	People in offices usually stand when they work.	True	False
2.	Sitting all day is bad for a person's health.	True	False
3.	When workers are sleepy, they make fewer mistakes.	True	False
4.	Some offices now have standing desks and walking desks.	True	False
5.	People need to use walking desks for the whole work day to be healthy.	True	False

Brands and Colors

Look around on the street. Do you see a lot of pictures or signs that make you think of businesses? It is a good thing for the businesses when people think of or
5 remember them easily. When they see a simple picture or a color and think of a company, the company has made a good brand.

Colors are important for good brands.
10 Red will make people think of love or of doing things. Blue makes people think of resting or trusting the brand. Yellow makes people think of happy things. And green makes people think of nature.

With all of the colors above, what kind of brands do you think of? Maybe red made you think of a shoe company. Maybe blue made you think of a bank. Or
15 maybe blue made you think of a travel company. Maybe yellow made you think of a restaurant, and green a garden business.

Now put two colors together, red and white. What is the first business that you think of? Is it a drink company? That is probably true for most people. The red-and-white brand for Coca-Cola is easy for more than 90% of the people all around the
20 world to remember.

Word Count 200 words

Time

Comprehension Questions

Circle the right answer.

1. This reading is about
   a. colors used by products and companies.
   b. people who choose expensive brands.
   c. the color that is best for advertising.

2. Which colors are NOT mentioned in the passage?
   a. Black and gold
   b. Blue and green
   c. Red and yellow

3. What is mentioned as a color that makes people think of nature?
   a. Blue
   b. Green
   c. Purple

4. Which color, according to the writer, would a restaurant use to give a happy and fun image?
   a. Red
   b. White
   c. Yellow

5. What is the product with an easily remembered red-and-white brand that is mentioned in the reading?
   a. A computer
   b. A drink
   c. A music store

 Score _____

Extra Practice

Circle the right word.

A brand is something like a 1. (fat / simple) picture or even a color that makes people think of a company. Sometimes, companies choose colors for their 2. (banks / brands) because the colors make people think of things or feel some way. Blue makes people think of resting, and it makes people feel 3. (nature / trust). This would be a good color for a 4. (travel / white) company's brand. Yellow is a happy color, so it might be a good color for the brand of a 5. (job / restaurant).

"HAPPY Birthday,"

Who Owns a Song?

It wouldn't be a birthday party without the song "Happy Birthday to You." It is the most well-known song in the English language. People all over the world know it and sing it. But did you ever wonder who owns that song?

It seems that the song was written by two school teachers in the US. The first
5 words were "Good morning to all." It was a nice, simple song that the children could sing each day. Later, the words were changed to "Happy birthday to you." This was in 1893. It wasn't until 1912 that the song was written down. But no one owned it.

In 1935, a company called Summy decided to try to be the owners of the song. They said that other people, not the two school teachers, wrote it. In 1988, the
10 Summy company was sold to a music company. The company said that anyone who wanted to sing "Happy Birthday to You" in public had to pay them. In September of 2015, it was decided by law that the song and the words could not be owned by anyone. So now "Happy Birthday to
15 You" is free for anyone to sing, at home or in public.

Word Count   200 words

 Time _____

Circle the right answer.

1. This reading is about
   a. what to do at a birthday.
   b. the history of a song.
   c. how song words have changed.

2. When was the song "Happy Birthday to You" made up?
   a. In the late 1800s
   b. In the 1930s
   c. In September of 2015

3. Who, according to the reading, made the song "Happy Birthday to You"?
   a. Two school children
   b. Two school teachers
   c. Two men who worked for Summy

4. How did Summy get the copyright to the song?
   a. They said something that was not true.
   b. They changed the words of the song.
   c. They clearly showed that they wrote it.

5. When can a person sing "Happy Birthday to You"?
   a. If it is at a private party and not recorded
   b. If he or she pays the Summy company
   c. Anywhere at any time

 Score _____

Extra Practice

Circle True or False for each sentence.

1. "Happy Birthday to You" is a well-known song in English.	True	False
2. This song was written by two teachers in the US.	True	False
3. The teachers changed the words from "happy birthday" to "good morning."	True	False
4. The Summy company paid the two teachers; then Summy owned the song.	True	False
5. Today, people must pay a music company when they sing this song.	True	False

Chapter 6 Food

A **Which place matches each of these facts? Write the country's name.**

1. People here eat sushi (raw fish on rice) and *inago* (a fried insect).

   _____

2. The world's hottest pepper is grown in this North American country.

   _____

3. This is where the British food called Marmite comes from.

   _____

4. Green tea was first made here thousands of years ago.

   _____

5. Farmers in this land between Japan and China grow a very spicy pepper.

   _____

B Choose the right word.

1. Cows need lots of _____ to walk around and eat grass.
   a. beer   b. land   c. pain

2. Green tea _____ many good things in it for your body.
   a. bites   b. contains   c. wastes

3. The company that made Marmite worked closely with a beer _____.
   a. company   b. bottle   c. insect

4. Small insects do not need a lot of _____ to live in.
   a. pepper   b. space   c. waste

5. The pepper that holds the world _____ for being the hottest pepper is from the US.
   a. chili   b. land   c. record

C Work with a classmate. Find out how often he or she. . .

	Often	Sometimes	Never
1. . . . cooks with a hot chili pepper or Habañero pepper.	☐	☐	☐
2. . . . eats in a restaurant that sells beer.	☐	☐	☐
3. . . . wastes food by throwing it away.	☐	☐	☐
4. . . . sees cooked insects for sale.	☐	☐	☐
5. . . . feels pain from biting his/her tongue.	☐	☐	☐

D Match each phrase to the right examples.

1. _____ Things you can drink
2. _____ World records
3. _____ Things you can eat
4. _____ Things that cause pain
5. _____ Things people waste

a. chili peppers, Marmite, insects
b. dog bites, fires, sharp things
c. the hottest pepper, the largest insect
d. land, money, time
e. water, tea, beer

Proper Nouns to Know

Study these words that you will find in the readings for this chapter.

| Australia | England | the United States | Habañero |

| China | New Zealand | Scoville heat units |

| Korea/Korean | Marmite | World War I |

Insects Are Good

Many people do not like insects. Insects do not look nice like a dog or cat. Insects also cause problems for us. They fly in

5   our houses. They also bite! So, many people kill them.

But what about insects as food? You may have never thought about eating insects, but much of the world already eats them.

10 However, people don't eat insects because they have to. They eat them because insects are good food.

Why should we eat insects? First, they are healthy! They have many of the things that people need every day. Second, insects are everywhere! There are 1,900 types of insects that are safe for people to eat and there are hundreds of each type. Even if everyone ate

15 insects, there would always be enough. That is because insects grow and spread fast. Third, insects are cheaper to raise than other types of food. They do not need to eat as much as a pig or a cow. And, they do not need much living space. That means that a lot of the land that is used now for pigs and cows could be used for other things.

Try eating an insect! You might like it!

Word Count 200 words

Time _____

Comprehension Questions

Circle the right answer.

1. This reading is about
   - a. why it is good to eat insects.
   - b. how to cook insects.
   - c. where to buy insects.

2. The writer says that many people think insects
   - a. are dirty.
   - b. cause problems.
   - c. are useless.

3. The number of people who eat insects is
   - a. a lot.
   - b. few.
   - c. none.

4. Which of the following is NOT mentioned as a benefit of eating insects?
   - a. They are easy to cook.
   - b. They are good for your health.
   - c. There are lots of them.

5. The reason most people eat insects is because
   - a. they think insects are good food.
   - b. they do not have enough food to eat.
   - c. they don't like to eat chicken or beef.

 Score _____

Extra Practice

Circle the right word.

People don't like insects because insects 1. (cause / own) problems and bite people. On the other hand, insects are good to eat. Many people around the world 2. (almost / already) eat them! Not only are insects easy to find everywhere, but they are also 3. (energy / healthy) to eat. Insects are also 4. (cheaper / worse) to raise than pigs and cows. They don't need much living space. Raising insects needs a lot less 5. (desk / land) than raising other animals to eat.

Green Tea

A lot of people are talking about green tea. This is because it really does help you stay well.

Green tea has been used in China for thousands of years. No one really knows the whole story about green tea. People say that the king of China began drinking
5   green tea thousands of years ago. It may have been used to make people feel better as early as 1000 BC. It was used for many types of health problems. Green tea was also used to help people feel less tired. However, people outside of China are just starting to understand the benefits of green tea.

Green tea has many different parts to it. These parts are all good for your
10 health. There are B vitamins in green tea. These kinds of vitamins help your body work well. Green tea also has something else in it that supports your good health.

Green tea has been shown to keep your mouth clean. It can also make your heart healthier.

Green tea contains something which makes you
15 feel less tired. But green tea is not like coffee. It is easier on your body. Try some green tea. You will be sure to like it.

Word Count   200 words

 **Time** _____

Circle the right answer.

1. This reading is about

    a. green tea and its benefits.

    b. green tea and the king of China.

    c. food made with green tea.

2. The writer says that

    a. green tea makes you tired.

    b. green tea might cause problems.

    c. green tea is good for you.

3. Which of the following is NOT mentioned as a good thing about green tea?

    a. Its color makes you feel less stress.

    b. Your heart is made healthier by green tea.

    c. Green tea can make you less tired.

4. When trying both coffee and green tea, you will find that green tea

    a. will give you less energy than coffee.

    b. is easier on your body.

    c. is much stronger than coffee.

5. Green tea has

    a. many different Chinese vitamins in it.

    b. nothing in it to help your mouth or teeth.

    c. different things that help your health.

 Score _____

Extra Practice

Circle True or False for each sentence.

1.	People in China have been drinking green tea for thousands of years.	True	False
2.	Chinese people drank green tea to feel better and feel less tired.	True	False
3.	People outside of China understood about green tea around 1000 BC.	True	False
4.	Green tea has things in it like vitamin B that support good health.	True	False
5.	Coffee is easier on your body than green tea.	True	False

Waste Not

Did you know that there are students who waste a lot of food? At one school, about 26% of the food was thrown away. Students were not just throwing away healthy food; they were also wasting water by wasting food. Farmers need to use a lot of water to grow the food we eat. Throwing away food is also bad for our world
5 because a lot of energy is used to move food from the farm to the stores.

There are ways not to waste food. One way to do this is to make your own food for school. Most students have little time to eat at school, so only bring the food you can eat in a short time. You should also only take as much food for lunch as you know you can eat.

10 A good way to stop wasting food is to get others to help you. At school, talk to teachers about food waste. Ask friends to see how much food is thrown away at school. Then start a group to help others understand
15 food waste. When the students and teachers all help, your school can cut down on food waste. This will save food and money.

Word Count 200 words

Time _____

Comprehension Questions

Circle the right answer.

1. This reading is about
   a. how students help waste.
   b. 26% of food being wasted.
   c. food waste in schools.

2. The writer says that
   a. it takes a lot of energy to grow apples.
   b. throwing away food wastes water.
   c. friends waste energy at school.

3. Which of the following is NOT mentioned as a way to stop wasting food?
   a. Use different kinds of energy to move food.
   b. Get others to understand food waste.
   c. Only take food you know you can eat.

4. If you want to stop food waste at school, you should
   a. eat out and share.
   b. ask other students to help.
   c. help farmers use less energy.

5. The writer says that at one school
   a. students had apples and watermelons.
   b. students did not throw away food.
   c. 26% of the food was wasted.

 Score _____

Extra Practice

Circle the right word.

When people throw away food, they are not just wasting 1. (healthy / smart) food. They are throwing away the water that 2. (farmers / scientists) used to grow the food. They are throwing away the energy that people used to 3. (contain / move) the food from farms to stores and homes. Students at school can talk about this problem with friends and teachers. When everyone 4. (mixes / understands) how much food is wasted, the school can cut down on what is thrown away. That will 5. (bite / save) both food and money.

Marmite

People in New Zealand and Australia love eating Marmite on bread. Marmite is a food with an interesting history. It was first made by a man living in England in the late 1800s. He found out that something used to

5 make beer could be used to put on food. In a few years, a company was formed to make Marmite. It worked with another company that made beer. Marmite became a well-known food in England.

During World War I, it was learned that

10 Marmite is good for you. It has a lot of vitamin B1. This was important. The people fighting in the war were getting sick. It was because they were not getting enough vitamin B1. So everyone who was fighting was given Marmite.

15 This kept them from getting sick and helped sick men get better.

Marmite has an unusual taste. So, people have strong feelings about it. They either love it or hate it. No one thinks that it is just OK. People talk about "the Marmite effect." That is when people have strong feelings on one side or other

20 about something. No one is in the middle. That is the Marmite effect. Do you like it?

Word Count   200 words

Comprehension Questions

Circle the right answer.

1. This reading is about
   a. ways of making beer.
   b. a popular food.
   c. World War I.

2. What is Marmite made from?
   a. Old beer that can't be sold in stores
   b. A food spread for sick people
   c. Something left when making beer

3. Why were men given Marmite in World War I?
   a. It had a lot of vitamin B1.
   b. It was not expensive.
   c. It could be kept a long time.

4. What is true about Marmite?
   a. Everyone seems to love it.
   b. No one just thinks it is OK.
   c. It makes young people sick.

5. What is an example of something that might create the Marmite effect?
   a. Something that people do not agree about
   b. A vitamin that people need
   c. A company that makes beer

 Score _____

Extra Practice

Circle True or False for each sentence.

1. Marmite was first made by a man in Australia.	True	False
2. Marmite was first made before World War I.	True	False
3. Marmite has vitamin B1 in it, so it is healthy for people to eat.	True	False
4. Everybody loves the strong taste of Marmite.	True	False
5. "The Marmite effect" means people are without strong feelings about something.	True	False

The Hotter, the Better

Pepper lovers don't love just any peppers. They love very hot peppers. The hotter the pepper, the better it is. And today's peppers just keep getting hotter.

Hot peppers come from the chili-pepper family. Chilies have something in them that makes the brain think that the mouth is really being burned. That is why a
5   hot pepper can cause pain in the mouth.

The "heat" of a pepper is measured in Scoville heat units (shu). A sweet pepper has zero shu. A very hot pepper from Korea can have 23,000 shu. Koreans will tell you it is very hot. But it is not hot enough for some people. They want their chilies even hotter, and pepper growers are
10   growing some really hot ones.

The contest to make the hottest chili is heating up. In the 1990s, the habañero was king. At 300,000 shu, it was the hottest pepper in the world. But pepper growers today are making even hotter chilies.
15   According to the world records, the hottest pepper now is from the United States. One of those peppers was tested at 2,200,000 shu!

These numbers don't stop pepper lovers, though. They will always be looking to find a
20   hotter pepper.

Word Count   200 words

Circle the right answer.

1. This reading is about
   a. hot places to visit.
   b. hot times of year.
   c. hot things to eat.

2. Which of these places is NOT listed in the reading as growing hot peppers?
   a. Australia
   b. The United States
   c. Korea

3. What is the heat of a pepper measured in?
   a. kph
   b. shu
   c. rpm

4. The pepper that holds the world record for heat
   a. is not the habañero.
   b. was first grown in Korea.
   c. looks like a sweet pepper.

5. The writer says that pepper lovers are always
   a. looking for better tasting peppers.
   b. looking for sweeter peppers.
   c. looking for hotter peppers.

 Score _____

Extra Practice

Circle the right word.

People are 1. (growing / wasting) peppers today that are hotter and hotter. Hot peppers, also called chilies, have something in them that makes your mouth feel like it is 2. (burning / tasting). Scientists can measure the "heat" of peppers using Scoville 3. (heat / sweet) units. In hot pepper 4. (beer / contests), the habeñero was the hottest pepper before. But the chili that holds the world 5. (record / type) for the hottest pepper today is much, much hotter than a habeñero!

Chapter 7 Sports

A **Match two phrases with each sport.**

a. play an electronic sport   b. drive a car   c. need an engine

d. kick and hit   e. like stacking blocks   f. use a computer

g. need skill to stack quickly   h. learn skills to protect yourself

1. Racing: _____ _____

2. Taekwondo: _____ _____

3. Cup Stacking: _____ _____

4. Gaming: _____ _____

B Write the right word in each blank. Two words will NOT be used.

better	electronic	protect	ready
rules	socks	team	stack

Some people who do sports put on special 1. _____ or touch their hats as they get 2. _____ to play. They believe these things help them do 3. _____ at their sport!

All sports have 4. _____ that players must follow, whether the player does the sport alone or on a 5. _____. The rules are there to 6. _____ all of the players.

C Answer these questions. Then ask your classmates. Can you find another person who has the same answers as you?

Name of other student

1. A boring sport to watch is _____. _____

2. A team sport that I sometimes enjoy is _____. _____

3. I don't know the rules of _____. _____

4. A fun electronic game I have played is _____. _____

D Find the right word in the box to add to the given words. Write the sports phrases below.

blocks	book	captain	engine	racing	socks

1. car _____ 2. soccer _____ 3. horse _____

4. stacking _____ 5. rule _____ 6. team _____

Proper Nouns to Know

Study these words that you will find in the readings for this chapter.

France   Korea   University of California, Irvine

Start Your Engines!

Motorsports are full of fast cars and fun! The sport of racing cars has a long history. People used to race cars on the roads from town to town. Car races started in the 1890s, and the first car race was in France. After that, people began to race their cars in other places, too. Racing cars on the road was very dangerous. People soon created closed tracks

5   so cars could race there without any problems. The first race cars were not very fast. They only went about 24 km/h. But some cars today can go as fast as 375 km/h.

The fastest cars are special kinds of race cars. They have only one seat, large tires, and no windows. The engine for the car is behind the driver, and the racing team has to build the car by themselves.

10   These cars race very fast. Many cars have their tires changed two or three times during the race. Drivers need to be strong and in good health to race, so they must exercise. They drink a lot of water before they race because the cars get very hot. Drivers can lose about 4 kg of water during a race.

Word Count   200 words

⏱ **Time**

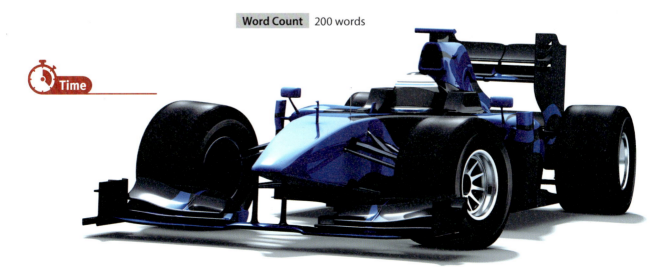

Comprehension Questions

Circle the right answer.

1. This reading is about
   a. how dangerous car racing is.
   b. a sport that uses cars.
   c. building a race car.

2. The writer says that
   a. racing on the streets is dangerous.
   b. racing on a closed track is not popular.
   c. racing cars is an expensive sport.

3. The first race cars only went
   a. about 24 km/h.
   b. about 375 km/h.
   c. about 4 km/h.

4. Which of the following is NOT part of the fastest race cars?
   a. A seat
   b. Windows
   c. Tires

5. In order to race, a driver must
   a. be in good health for a race.
   b. not drink water before or during a race.
   c. drive with another person in the car.

 Score _____

Extra Practice

Circle True or False for each sentence.

1.	The first car race was in Germany.	True	False
2.	The first cars went less than 30 km/h.	True	False
3.	Today, cars can race at over 300 km/h.	True	False
4.	The fastest race cars have no seats or windows.	True	False
5.	Today, race cars only need to change their tires after races.	True	False

Cup Stacking

Can you quickly put a cup on top of other cups to make a special shape? If so, you can be a stacker!

Children all over the world are doing sport stacking. In sport stacking, or cup stacking, you must quickly place cups one on top of the other in the right order.

5 There are three ways to make these stacks, and the easiest way is called the 3-3-3. In the 3-3-3, nine cups are made into three stacks, with two cups on the bottom and one cup on top. After making the stacks, you have to take them down again. More cups can be added to make the stacks of cups much higher.

10 Cup stacking is a lot like building with blocks, but you need to build very fast. Cup stacking is good for you, too. It helps your eyes and hands work together. It also helps you move much more quickly. Cup stacking helps you use both sides of your brain. Cup stacking may also help
15 you learn how to read better.

It seems that cup stacking can help students in many ways. But what is the most important thing about cup stacking? It is a lot of fun!

Word Count   200 words

Circle the right answer.

1. This reading is about
   a. why children don't like cup stacking.
   b. how to win at cup stacking.
   c. what cup stacking is.

2. The writer says that the most important thing about cup stacking is
   a. that it makes you stack in order.
   b. that it helps you win money.
   c. that it is fun for you to do.

3. After you put the cups in a stack, you have to
   a. take them down.
   b. remember them.
   c. run to your team.

4. Which of the following is NOT mentioned as a good thing about cup stacking?
   a. Cup stacking makes you a better reader.
   b. Your hands and eyes work together.
   c. You can meet kids from all over the world.

5. The easiest way to stack is
   a. in a 3-3-3 stack.
   b. using special sport cups.
   c. with cups and building blocks.

 Score _____

Extra Practice

Circle the right word.

One kind of sport stacking is 1. (car / cup) stacking. In this sport, a person must 2. (dangerously / quickly) stack the cups that they are given. An easy way to do this is 3-3-3 stacking with three stacks of two cups on the 3. (bottom / front) and one on the top. Cup stacking is a lot like building towers with 4. (blocks / engines). Like building with blocks, this kind of exercise makes a person use both sides of his or her 5. (brain / team).

Kicking for Fun

Taekwondo is a fun sport. It helps your body and mind. The word "taekwondo" is made up of three smaller words. When you put these smaller words together, they say taekwondo is like "the way of the foot and hand." These ways of kicking and hitting were known in Korea in 50 BC. The taekwondo we know today uses

5   these old kicks and hits. It has some other things, too. Taekwondo is a way to use your body to protect yourself. It also helps you get some exercise. It takes a lot of practice to do the kicks in taekwondo. You have to exercise every day.

But taekwondo is not just about kicking or hitting. It is not even just about exercising. It is about how you think. To do taekwondo well, you must think in a

10   special way. There are rules for how to think. These rules were important to how taekwondo came to be. Some of these rules are about how to respect other people. Some of these rules are about how to act. "Share" and "Be honest" are important rules. One of the most important rules is to not give up. This is important when you need to practice!

Word Count   200 words

🕐 **Time** _____

Comprehension Questions

Circle the right answer.

1. This reading is about
   a. when taekwondo started in Korea.
   b. how taekwondo uses both your body and mind.
   c. why taekwondo teaches you to be honest.

2. The writer says that
   a. taekwondo is only for exercise.
   b. it is fun to share and be honest.
   c. you need to practice every day.

3. Some of the kicks from taekwondo
   a. were known in Korea in 50 BC.
   b. teach you how to act.
   c. are not for protecting yourself.

4. Which of the following is NOT part of the rules for taekwondo?
   a. Being honest
   b. Being respectful
   c. Being quick

5. What is one of the most important rules in taekwondo?
   a. Be in good health.
   b. Do not give up.
   c. Use small words.

 Score _____

Extra Practice

Circle True or False for each sentence.

1. Taekwondo helps a person's body and mind.	True	False
2. This sport came from Korea.	True	False
3. Taekwondo uses kicking but not hitting.	True	False
4. Taekwondo can help you protect yourself.	True	False
5. An important rule in taekwondo is to be honest.	True	False

Believe It or Not

Many people who play sports try things to help them do well. Some of these things do help them, like practicing. The more you practice, the better you will be.

5　But some things don't have anything to do with how well you play. Some examples are wearing special socks or touching your hat before you play. Of course, your socks or hat are not going to make you play better. But you believe that they will. And sometimes that is enough.

10　Because a player believes it, it works.

Believing that one thing causes another when really it does not is usually not good. However, in sports it can help. It can help players get their minds ready for the game. It can be part of some steps to keep their minds on the game. But it can cause problems as well. For example, a player might believe she needs special socks

15　in order to play well. Those socks could get lost. Then the thing that helped her feel good about herself is gone. It could change the way she thinks about the game. Then she might not play her best. Players need to believe in themselves, not in their socks.

Word Count　200 words

Comprehension Questions

Circle the right answer.

1. This reading is about
   a. how to be better at sports through practice.
   b. how well a player does is affected by his or her thinking.
   c. how believing the wrong thing can be bad for players.

2. What is mentioned as something all players do that helps them to play better?
   a. Practicing their sport
   b. Trusting other players
   c. Eating a healthy diet

3. How can a belief help a sports player?
   a. The player will get a special job on the team.
   b. The player will believe he or she will do well.
   c. Some of the player's stress will be taken away.

4. How can a belief about socks or hats be bad for players?
   a. By making players think how well they play comes from these things
   b. By taking players' eyes off the other players on the team
   c. By pushing players not to practice as much as they should

5. What does the writer think about what players believe in sports?
   a. There are false beliefs, and players should not hold them.
   b. Some beliefs can be helpful as long as the players know what is real.
   c. All strong beliefs can help players do better at their sports.

 Score _____

Extra Practice

Circle the right word.

> Some people have to do special things 1. (before / order) they play a sport. They think these things will help them play 2. (better / important). Maybe these people put on special 3. (rules / socks) or always touch their hats. Do these things really work? They might help someone get his or her mind 4. (racing / ready) for the game. But if a person 5. (believes / causes) he or she can't play without doing these things, then it is a problem!

The No-Sweat Sport

What games come to mind when you think about sports? Probably basketball or soccer. Well, there are new kinds of sports growing in the world these days. They are electronic sports, better known as Esports. Esports are computer games. People play these games against each other to see who is the best. But people are not sure
5 if playing computer games is a real sport or not.

Some people say that Esports are not real sports. The biggest reason is that when you play Esports, you do not have to move much. For example, there is no running or jumping. Most gamers do not get quickly tired when playing Esports. Still, others will say that Esports are like any other sport. First, skill and thinking are
10 needed in Esports, just like in any other sport. Second, a lot of time and practice are needed to be good at Esports.

Who says Esports are real sports, and who says they are not? The University of California in Irvine says they are. This
15 university started letting Esports players in to play for their university. On the other hand, people like the president of ESPN sports television say Esports are still not a sport.

Word Count 200 words

 Time _____

Circle the right answer.

1. This reading is about
   a. how much money Esports gamers make.
   b. if Esports are real sports or not.
   c. Esports that young people do.

2. The writer says that Esports are another name for
   a. everyday sports.
   b. everybody's sport.
   c. electronic sports.

3. Which of the following is NOT mentioned as a part of normal sports?
   a. Sitting
   b. Jumping
   c. Running

4. Esports require
   a. big muscles.
   b. quick feet.
   c. knowing how to win.

5. The University of California in Irvine
   a. does not allow Esports.
   b. pays for Esports competitions.
   c. has Esport players at their university.

 Score _____

Extra Practice

Circle True or False for each sentence.

1.	More and more people are playing Esports these days.	True	False
2.	People agree that Esports are real sports.	True	False
3.	People don't have to move much when they play Esports.	True	False
4.	Like in other sports, skill and thinking are needed in Esports.	True	False
5.	No universities in the US let Esports players into their schools.	True	False

A Look at the pictures. Write the right words.

cello	created	fixes	guy
instruments	piano	star	windmill

1. The _____ is broken. It might work if someone _____ it.

2. This _____ is a musician. He knows how to play the _____.

3. Someone _____ an interesting work of art here. It is made from musical _____.

4. The man playing the _____ is famous. He is the _____ of the show.

B Circle the right answer.

1. Which instrument can one person carry?   A cello   A piano
2. Which generation was born after 2000?   Baby Boomers   Generation Z
3. Where would a person probably find a good book?   In a library   In a windmill
4. What might you call the best player on a team?   The prize player   The star player
5. Who is more likely to use beauty products?   A girl   A guy

C Work with a group of classmates. Ask and answer these questions.

1. Which instrument is harder to learn, the piano or the cello? Why do you think so?
2. When did you last visit a library? What did you do there?
3. What kind of beauty products are in your home? Who uses them?
4. Where might people want to build windmills?
5. Are you more interested in news stories about stars who are guys or stars who are girls?

D Match the phrases to the right examples.

1. _____ Things in a library   a. beauty, talent, luck
2. _____ Different kinds of prizes   b. books, magazines, newspapers
3. _____ Musical instruments   c. create, fix, imagine
4. _____ Things that stars need   d. engines, windmills, the sun
5. _____ Things that make or give power e. money, ribbons, gold cups
6. _____ What smart people can do   f. pianos, cellos, drums

Proper Nouns to Know

Study these words that you will find in the readings for this chapter.

Brazil   Hollywood   Malawi

Marta Vieira da Silva   Michelle Phan

Steven Sharp Nelson   William Kamkwamba   YouTube

Go, Marta!

Marta Vieira Da Silva is one of the best soccer players in the world. Many people watch her games and think she is a great player. They call her by her first name, Marta. She was born in 1986 in Brazil into a family with three brothers and sisters. Her family was very poor. Marta started playing sports when she was very young. She liked to play with the

5   other children in the street. People saw that Marta could be a great soccer player. She was asked to join a special team when she was just 14 years old. Marta can play different places in the team and does well

10 in all of them. She is very fast and thinks quickly.

Marta has played soccer all around the world. She has played for nine soccer teams. She usually plays on teams with only women, but one time, she played on a team

15 with men. Marta won a number of prizes. She won World Player of the Year five times! She also has the world record for the most points—15—at the Women's World Cup. Today, Marta still plays soccer. But she also tries to help other women in the world.

Word Count   200 words

Comprehension Questions

Circle the right answer.

1. This reading is about
   a. how a person can win many soccer awards.
   b. a poor woman who became a great soccer player.
   c. a woman from Brazil who watches games.

2. Which of the following is NOT mentioned as something Marta has done?
   a. She once played on a team with men.
   b. She once played in the street.
   c. She once played in the Men's World Cup.

3. The writer says that Marta
   a. joined a special team when she was 14 years old.
   b. played soccer when she was 3 years old.
   c. was part of fifteen soccer groups.

4. Which of the following is NOT mentioned about how Marta plays?
   a. She plays best when her family watches her.
   b. She can play many places on the team.
   c. She is very fast and thinks quickly.

5. The writer says that Marta now
   a. is a part of nine soccer groups.
   b. plays every World Cup.
   c. helps other women.

 Score _____

Extra Practice

Circle the right word.

> Marta Vieira Da Silva is one of the best 1. (soccer / sport) players in the world. She was 2. (born / great) in 1986 in Brazil. When she was young, she played soccer in the street with her friends. She was asked to join a special 3. (prize / team) when she was 14. Now she is one of the 4. (best / five) women's soccer players in the world. She has the world 5. (place / record) for the most points in the Women's World Cup.

William's Windmills

William Kamkwamba was a poor child in Malawi. His family had a farm where they grew food. But then there was no rain for a long time. Food wasn't growing. His parents did not have money to send him to school. He had to stop going to school. But he wanted to keep learning. He went to the library a lot. From books,

5   he learned how to fix radios. He got a little bit of money doing that, but not much. Then he read a book about windmills. He got the idea to make one.

Using just wood, bike parts, and other things he found, he built a

10   windmill. It was strong enough to power a few things in his family's home. He was only 15. Many people around the world became interested in his story. He was asked to speak to large groups of

15   people. Some of the people he spoke to wanted to help him. They gave him money to go to university. William has built more windmills and also a tool for moving water that is powered by the sun. He has also written a book, and there is a movie about him, *William and the*

20   *Windmill.*

Word Count   200 words

Circle the right answer.

1. This reading is about
   a. a man who made a new kind of wind machine.
   b. how a boy became famous for making something.
   c. the problems faced by a poor boy in school.

2. Why did William Kamkwamba stop going to school?
   a. Because his parents could not pay for school
   b. So that he could spend more time at the library
   c. In order to work in his new job of making clean energy

3. What was NOT mentioned as something used in William's first windmill?
   a. Wood
   b. Clothes
   c. Bike parts

4. What did William Kamkwamba's first windmill power?
   a. A machine for getting water
   b. Some things in his family's home
   c. Lights at the library in his town

5. What is NOT mentioned as something William has done since building his first windmill?
   a. Go to university
   b. Write a book
   c. Star in a movie

 Score _____

Extra Practice

Circle True or False for each sentence.

1. William Kamkwamba was born in Malawi.	True	False
2. His family ran a school.	True	False
3. William liked to go to the library.	True	False
4. William built a bike using parts of a windmill.	True	False
5. William wrote a movie about his country.	True	False

Making Beautiful Music

The Piano Guys are famous for their music. There are four people in the group. Their cello player is Steven Sharp Nelson. He began playing the cello when he was around seven years old. Now, he owns many unusual musical instruments. He also plays the cello in very interesting ways. Sometimes, he even hits the cello to make
5   music.

Steven can play many different instruments, and he likes all kinds of music. Steven's mom was a singer. Steven's dad taught him how to love music. He says that his dad and mom helped him a lot in his life.

10   Learning new things has never been easy for Steven. Like some kids in schools today, Steven has a hard time thinking about one thing for a long time. This makes practicing the cello very difficult.

But Steven has learned about ways to help
15   himself. He practices for a while and then takes a break before practicing again. He also tries to do different things at the same time. While he plays the cello, he sometimes plays another instrument, too! Steven has not let his problem slow him down or
20   stop him from playing. He still works hard writing and playing music.

Time

Word Count   200 words

Circle the right answer.

1. This reading is about
   a. famous cello players and their instruments.
   b. a cello player with a problem.
   c. a guy who made a new kind of piano.

2. The writer says that
   a. Steven has unusual instruments.
   b. Steven can play any music he hears.
   c. Steven can play only the piano.

3. Which of the following is NOT mentioned as a way that Steven helps himself?
   a. He takes breaks while practicing.
   b. When he practices, he does so for a long time.
   c. He plays different instruments at the same time.

4. Steven says that his mom and dad
   a. have helped him a lot.
   b. are part of the Piano Guys.
   c. made his music famous.

5. Steven began playing the cello
   a. when he joined the Piano Guys.
   b. when he saw one in a movie.
   c. when he was around seven years old.

 Score _____

Extra Practice

Circle the right word.

The Piano Guys are 1. (difficult / famous) for their music. Their 2. (cello / team) player is Steven Sharp Nelson. Steven has a kind of 3. (problem / record) that makes it hard for him to think about one thing for a long time. Steven takes breaks when he practices, or he plays the cello and another 4. (instrument / library) at the same time. Steven has not let his problem slow him down or 5. (join / stop) him from playing.

An Internet Star

They do not act. But they are in videos watched by lots of people. They are not famous in Hollywood. But they are stars. Who are these people? They are YouTube stars.

5 YouTube was created in 2005. It is a place where people can share videos that they have made. If a lot of people watch a video, the video creators can make lots of money. How? Every video has an advertisement with it. Google takes some of the money from these
10 advertisements. The creator of the video takes the rest of the money.

Michelle Phan was one of the first to become rich and well-known as a YouTube star. From 2007, she has created beauty videos on YouTube. For example,
15 she shows people how to look beautiful and take care of their skin. She also gives beauty advice and talks about beauty ideas. She has made more than 300 videos and has nearly 9 million followers. Her videos have been viewed more than 1 billion times! From YouTube videos alone, Michelle gets about $15,000 every month.

If you want to share something with the world, share it on YouTube. You could
20 end up being an internet star like Michelle Phan!

Word Count 200 words

Time

Comprehension Questions

Circle the right answer.

1. This reading is about
   a. a famous person in movies.
   b. a famous YouTube star.
   c. a famous website company.

2. YouTube allows people
   a. to share videos.
   b. to share pictures.
   c. to share homework.

3. What does Michelle Phan put up on the internet?
   a. Advertisements
   b. Beauty lessons
   c. Family stories

4. Which of the following is NOT mentioned as receiving advertisement money?
   a. Video creators
   b. Google
   c. YouTube followers

5. Through YouTube, Michelle Phan earns about
   a. $3,000/video.
   b. $15,000/month.
   c. $900,000/year.

 Score _____

Extra Practice

Circle True or False for each sentence.

1. YouTube stars are video stars, but they don't have to be in Hollywood.	True	False
2. Only famous people can share videos on YouTube.	True	False
3. Michelle Phan has created beauty videos on YouTube.	True	False
4. Michelle gives advice and ideas to people through her videos.	True	False
5. She has made 9 million videos and makes $1 billion every month.	True	False

Born to Be the Same?

A generation is all the people born around the same time. People of each generation live in the world together at the same time. So, each generation's view of the world is usually much the same.

5 Generation X are people who were born in the 1960s and 1970s. During this time, both parents of many families worked outside the home. Children would stay at home alone after school until their parents returned. In some ways, this may be why people in generation X can usually take care of themselves.

Generation Y are those born in the 1980s and 1990s. Like generation X, the people of generation Y grew up with hard-working parents. However, they are
10 sometimes called the "me" generation because they think about themselves first. However, they are usually open to new ideas.

Generation Z or the "I generation" are those who were born after the mid-1990s. They have never known a world without the internet. They have smartphones and use the internet a lot. They are the most connected generation.
15 Through the internet, they learn about difficulties and money problems around the world. So, it is thought that it will be generation Z that brings about good change.

Word Count 200 words

Time

Comprehension Questions

Circle the right answer.

1. This reading is about
   a. different types of generations.
   b. things that don't change over time.
   c. generations in one family.

2. The writer says that a generation is made up of people who
   a. are born around the same time.
   b. die at the same time.
   c. live in the same country.

3. What is Generation Y also known as?
   a. The sport generation
   b. The I generation
   c. The me generation

4. Generation Z includes people born in the
   a. 1960s.
   b. 1980s.
   c. 1990s.

5. The writer says that the I Generation is
   a. the most connected generation.
   b. the richest generation.
   c. the oldest generation.

 Score _____

Extra Practice

Circle the right word.

Each generation's 1. (skin / view) of the world is usually much the same. The children of generation X stayed at home 2. (alone / born) after school while their parents were at work. They know how to take 3. (advice / care) of themselves. Generation Y is called the "me" 4. (generation / prize) because they think about themselves a lot. The I generation has never known a world without the internet. They are the most 5. (born / connected) generation.

Reading Speed Chart

Reading Speed Chart

Write your score for each reading passage at the bottom of the chart. Then put an X in one of the boxes above the reading passage number to mark your time for each passage. Look on the right side of the chart to find your reading speed for each reading passage.

Time																					wpm
45s																					266
50s																					240
55s																					218
1m																					200
1m 5s																					185
1m 10s																					171
1m 15s																					160
1m 20s																					150
1m 25s																					141
1m 30s																					133
1m 35s																					126
1m 40s																					120
1m 45s																					114
1m 50s																					109
1m 55s																					104
2m																					100
2m 5s																					96
2m 10s																					92
2m 15s																					89
2m 20s																					85
2m 25s																					83
2m 30s																					80
Reading	1	2	3	4	5	6	7	8	9	10	11	12	13	14	15	16	17	18	19	20	
Score																					

Reading Speed Chart

Write your score for each reading passage at the bottom of the chart. Then put an X in one of the boxes above the reading passage number to mark your time for each passage. Look on the right side of the chart to find your reading speed for each reading passage.

Time																					wpm
45s																					266
50s																					240
55s																					218
1m																					200
1m 5s																					185
1m 10s																					171
1m 15s																					160
1m 20s																					150
1m 25s																					141
1m 30s																					133
1m 35s																					126
1m 40s																					120
1m 45s																					114
1m 50s																					109
1m 55s																					104
2m																					100
2m 5s																					96
2m 10s																					92
2m 15s																					89
2m 20s																					85
2m 25s																					83
2m 30s																					80
Reading	21	22	23	24	25	26	27	28	29	30	31	32	33	34	35	36	37	38	39	40	
Score																					